BEGINNING PIANO SOLO

10 FUN FAVORITES

ISBN 978-1-4768-7553-8

HAL•LEONARD® CORPORATION

7777 W. BLUEMOUND RD. P.O. BOX 13819 MILWAUKEE, WI 53213

Visit Hal Leonard Online at
www.halleonard.com

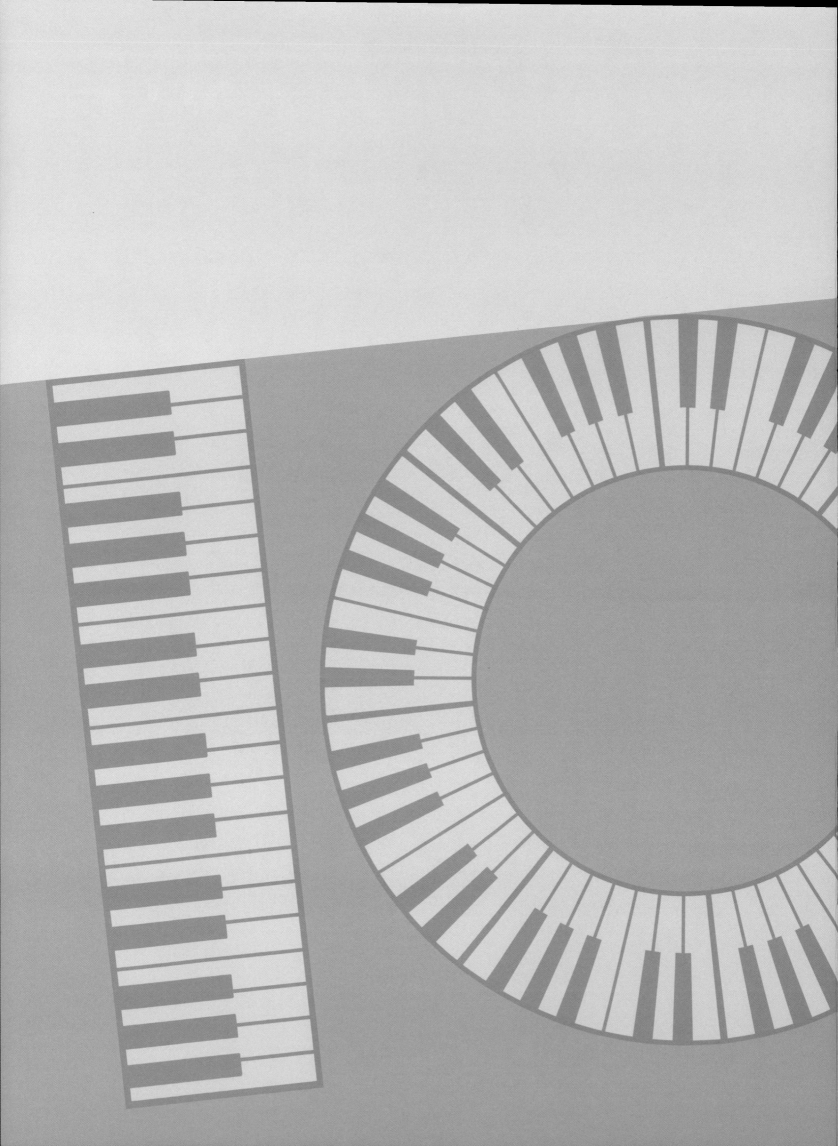

CATCH A FALLING STAR

Words and Music by PAUL VANCE
and LEE POCKRISS

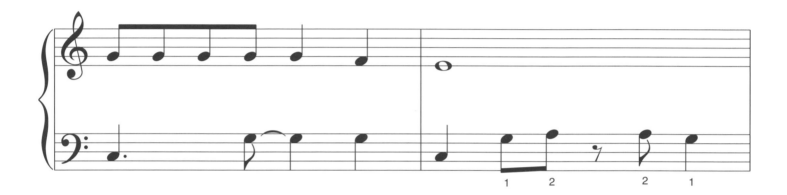

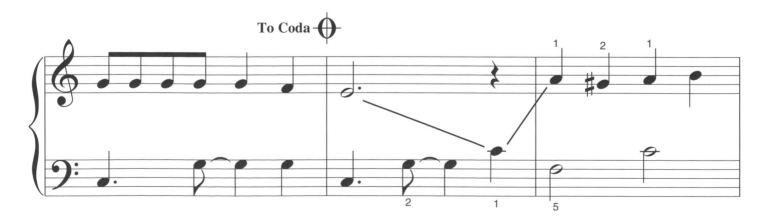

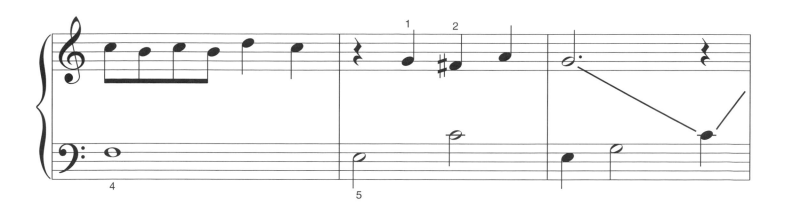

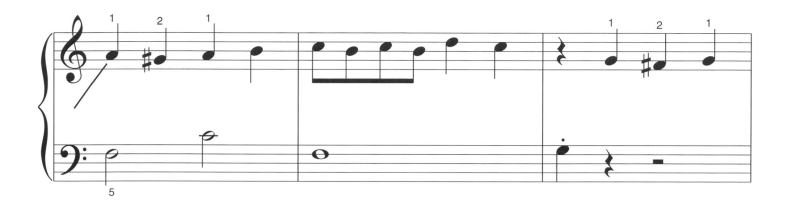

D.C. al Coda

CODA

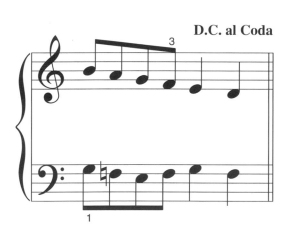

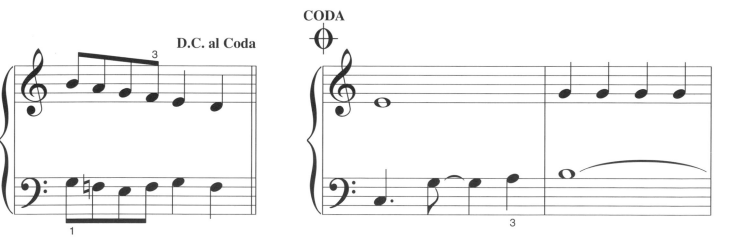

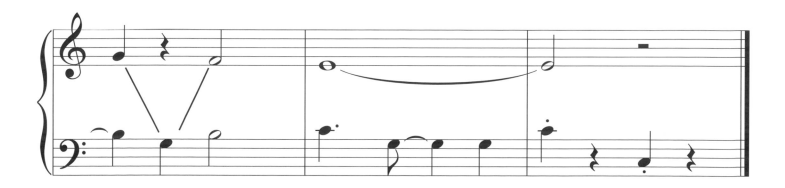

HAPPY BIRTHDAY TO YOU

Words and Music by MILDRED J. HILL
and PATTY S. HILL

Grandly, in 1

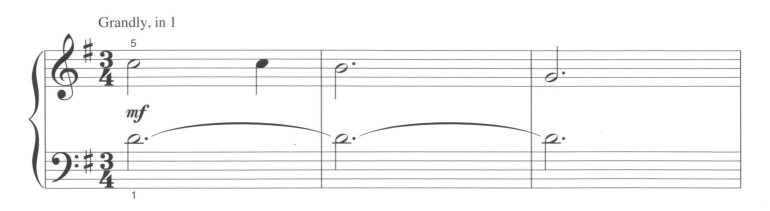

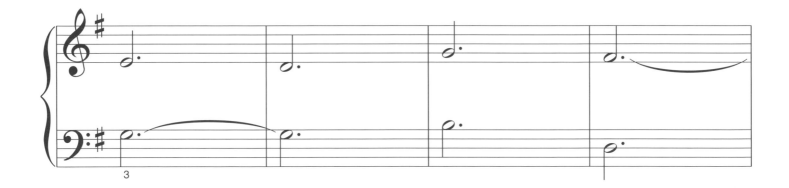

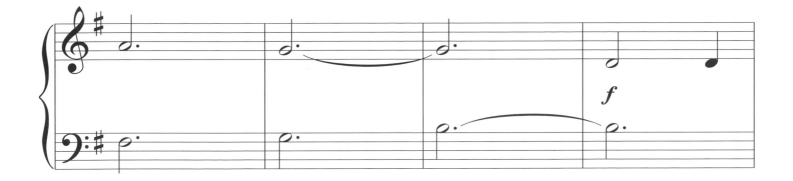

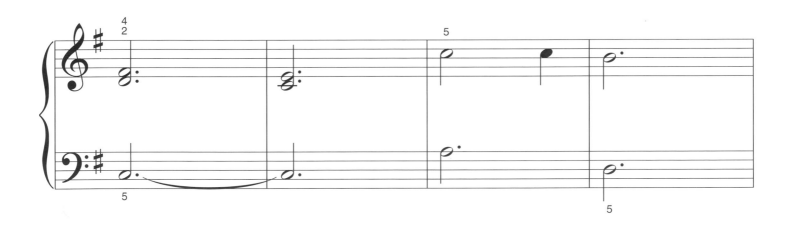

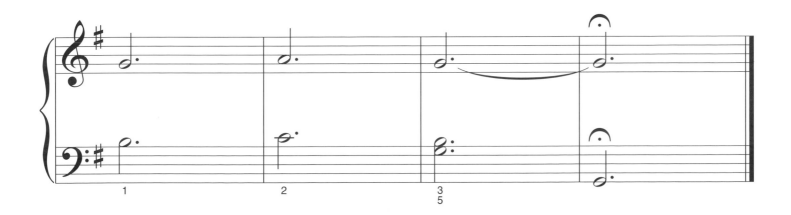

THE HOKEY POKEY

Words and Music by CHARLES P. MACAK,
TAFFT BAKER and LARRY LaPRISE

Brightly

TOMORROW

from the Musical Production ANNIE

Lyric by MARTIN CHARNIN
Music by CHARLES STROUSE

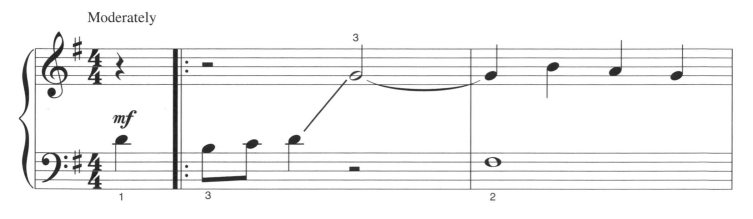

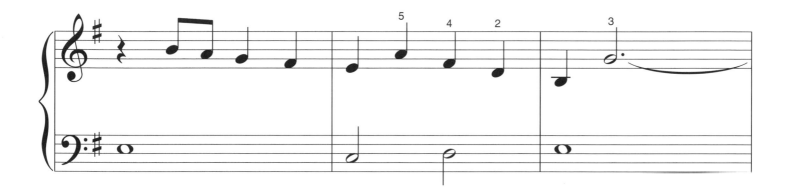

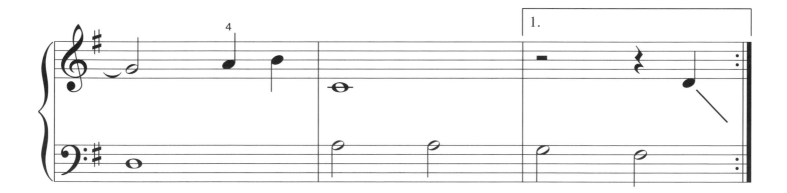

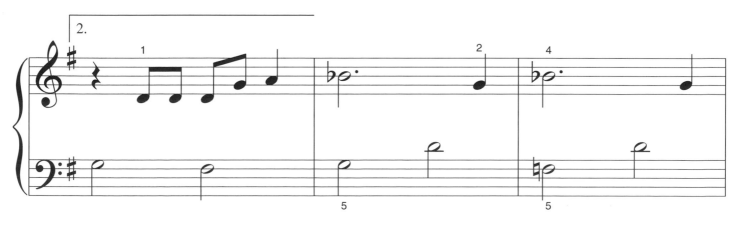

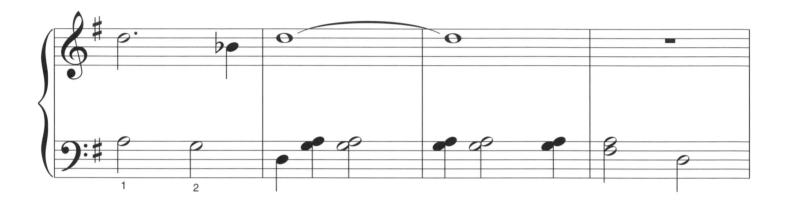

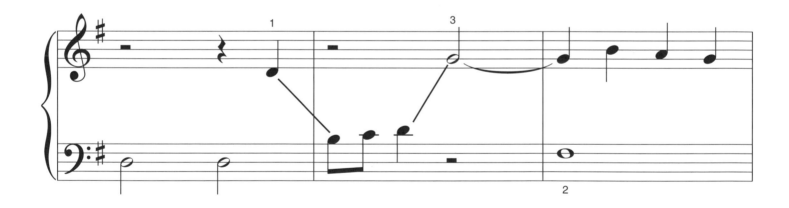

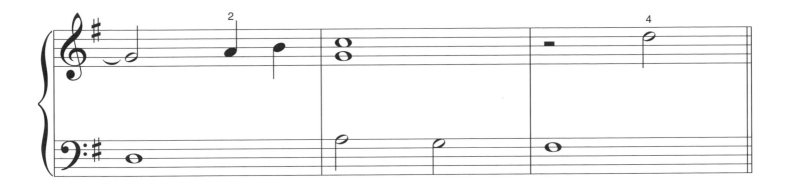

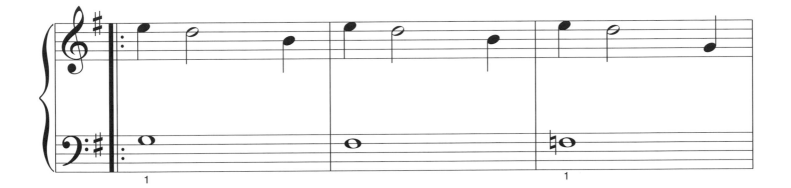

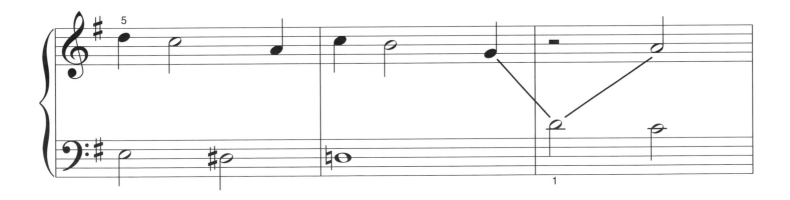

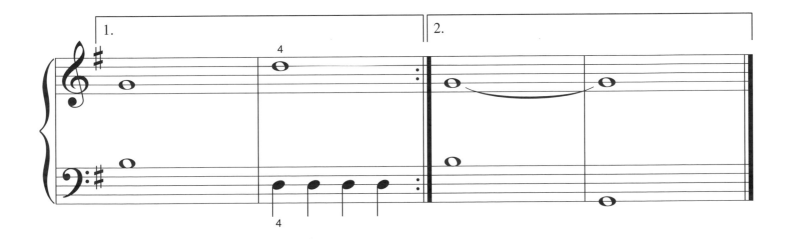

I'D LIKE TO TEACH THE WORLD TO SING

Words and Music by BILL BACKER,
ROQUEL DAVIS, ROGER COOK
and ROGER GREENAWAY

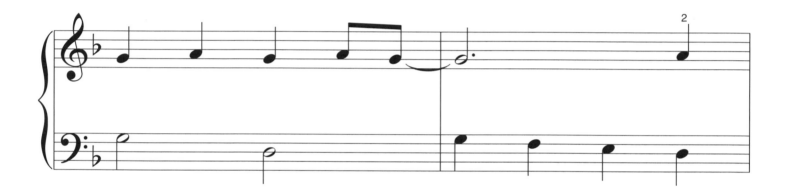

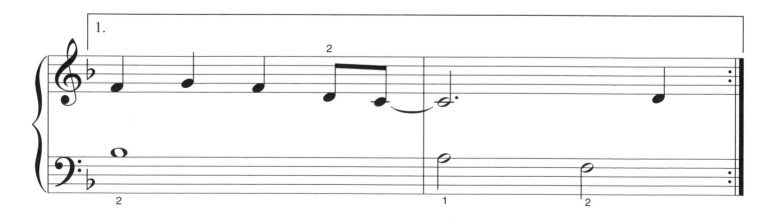

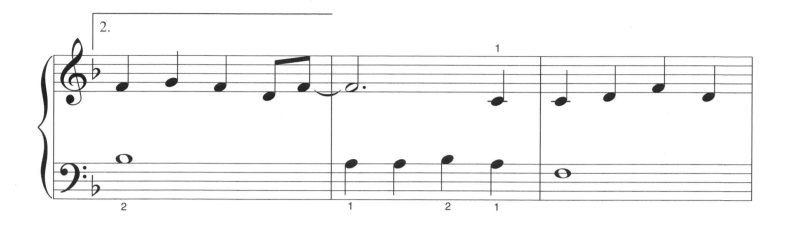

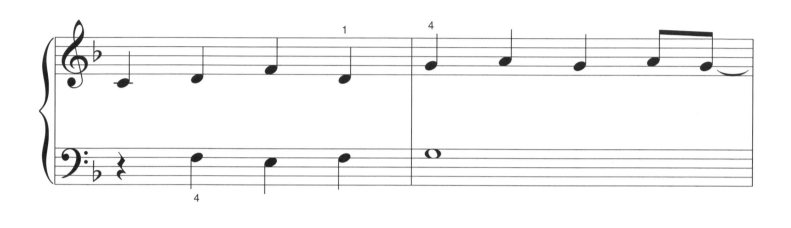

I'M AN OLD COWHAND
(From the Rio Grande)

Words and Music by
JOHNNY MERCER

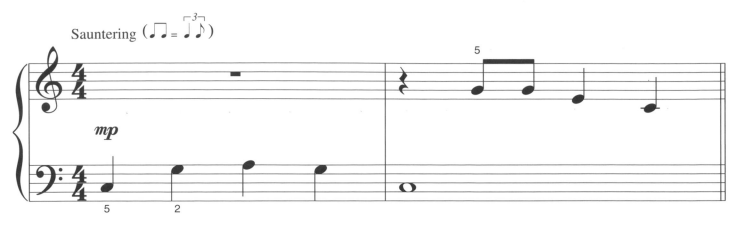

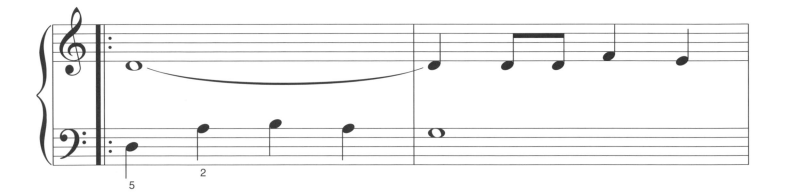

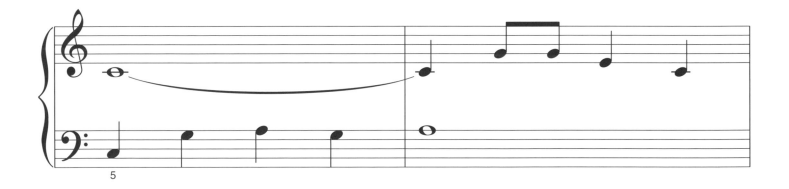

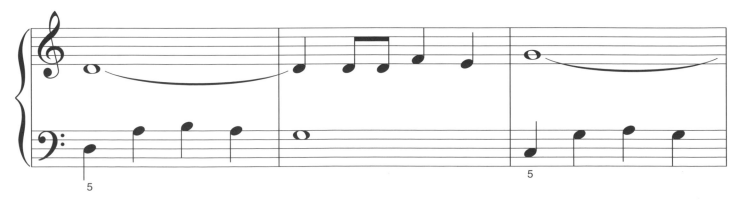

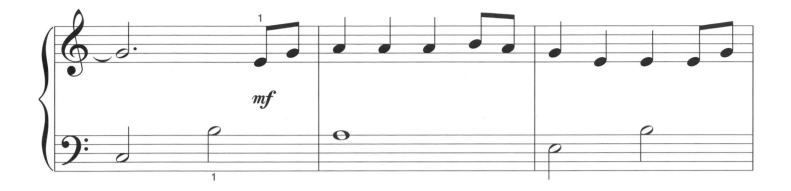

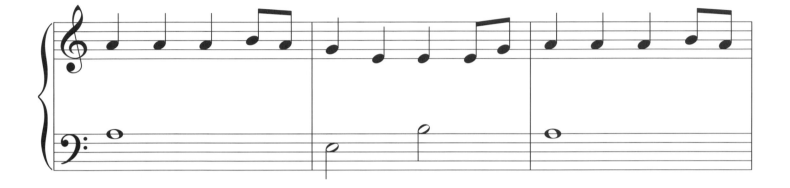

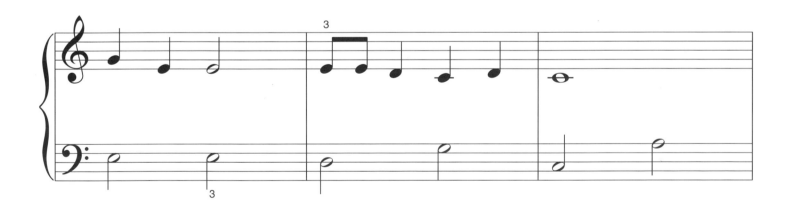

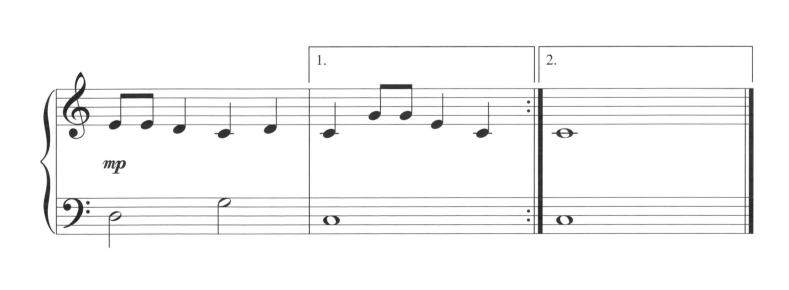

LET IT BE

Words and Music by JOHN LENNON
and PAUL McCARTNEY

Slowly

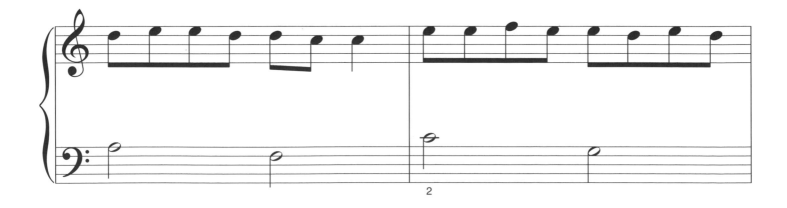

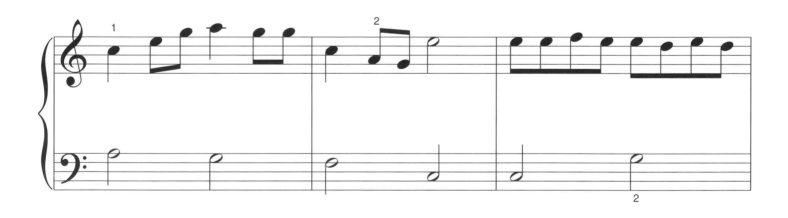

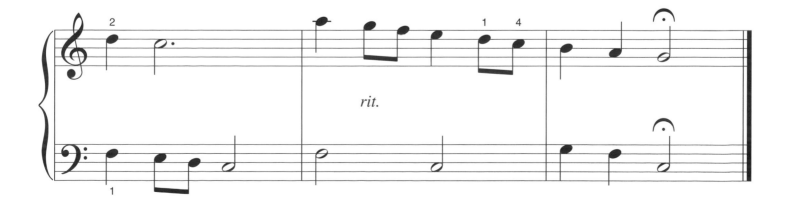

OVER THE RAINBOW

from THE WIZARD OF OZ

Music by HAROLD ARLEN
Lyric by E.Y. "YIP" HARBURG

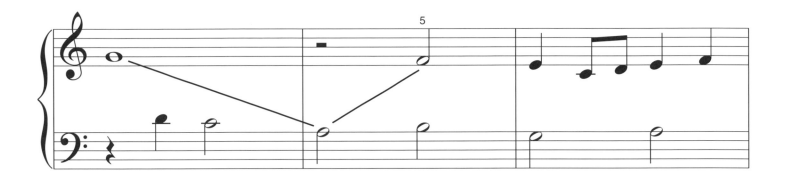

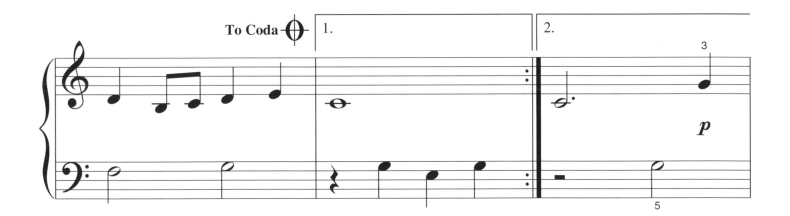

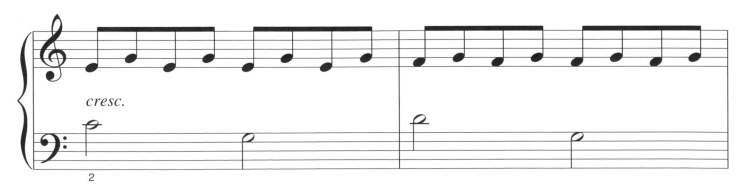

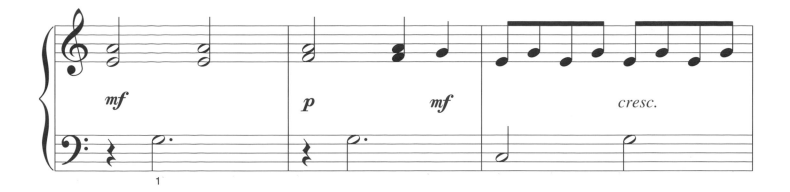

D.C. al Coda

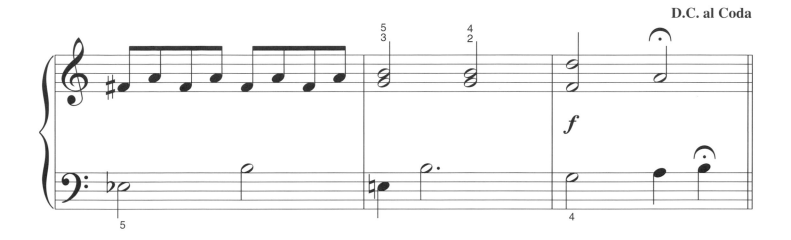

CODA

STAR WARS
(Main Theme)
from STAR WARS, THE EMPIRE STRIKES BACK and RETURN OF THE JEDI

Music by JOHN WILLIAMS

Majestically

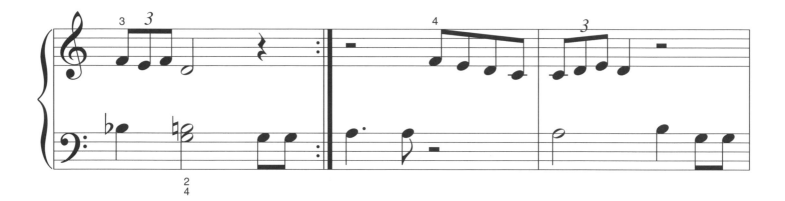

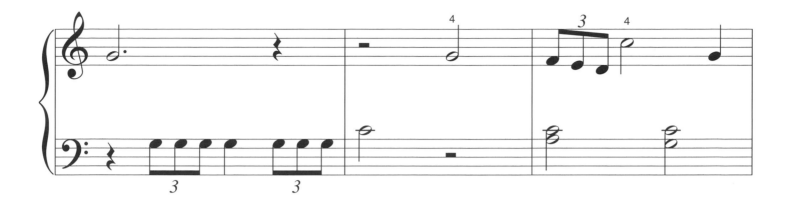

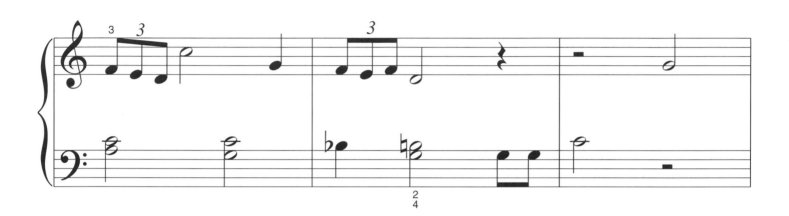

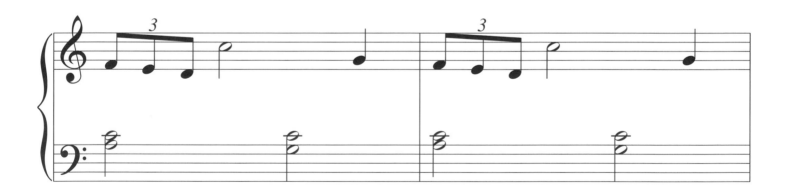

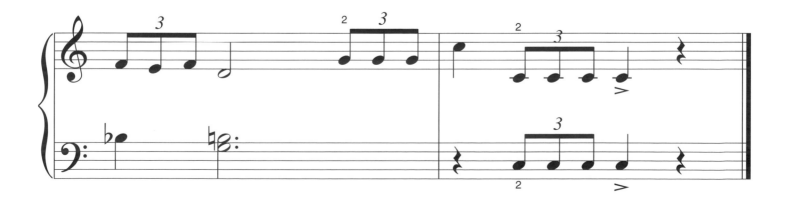

WHAT A WONDERFUL WORLD

Words and Music by GEORGE DAVID WEISS
and BOB THIELE

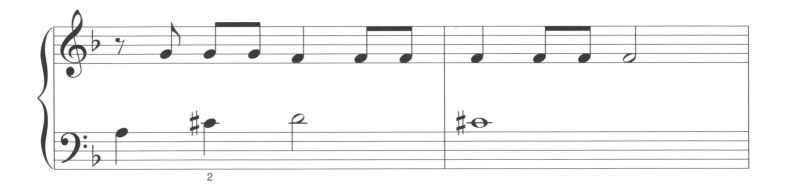

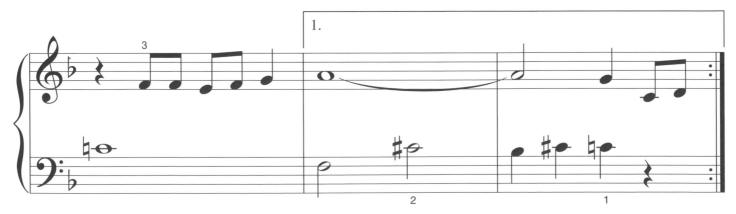

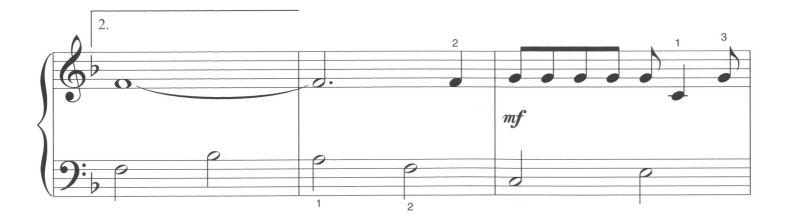

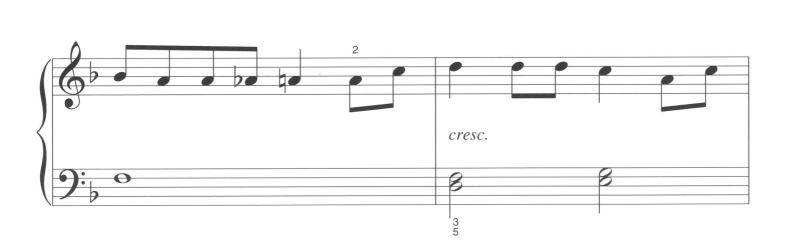

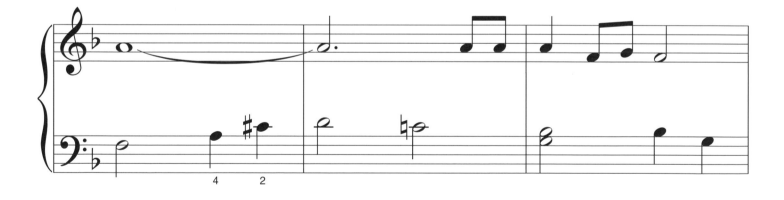